ANIMAL CHARACTERS

ANIMAL CHARACTERS
An alphabet by Jean Christian Knaff

Picture Book Studio

© 1987 JEAN CHRISTIAN KNAFF

FIRST PUBLISHED IN GREAT BRITAIN BY FABER & FABER LIMITED, LONDON.
PUBLISHED IN USA BY PICTURE BOOK STUDIO LTD, NATICK, MA.

PRINTED IN GREAT BRITAIN BY W.S. COWELL LTD, IPSWICH.

LIBRARY OF CONGRESS CATALOGING IN PUBLICATION DATA:

KNAFF, JEAN CHRISTIAN.   ANIMAL CHARACTERS.

SUMMARY: TWENTY-SIX ANIMALS ARE PICTURED
WITH THE LETTERS OF THE ALPHABET.

1. ENGLISH LANGUAGE – ALPHABET – JUVENILE LITERATURE.
2. ANIMALS – JUVENILE LITERATURE.
[1. ANIMALS – PICTORIAL WORKS. 2. ALPHABET]   I. TITLE.
PE1155.K6 1988   421'.1 [E]   87-7290
ISBN 0-88708-055-3

For Anton

A1LIGATOR

BABOON

CAMEL

DODO

ELEPHANT

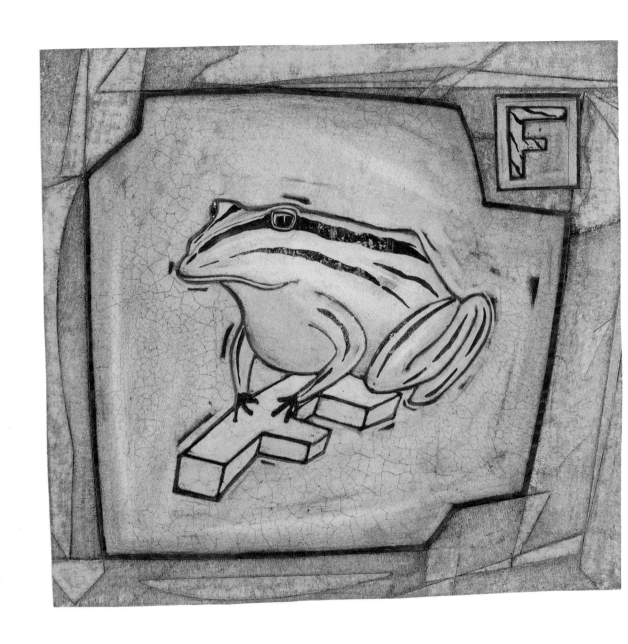

FROG

GIRAFFE

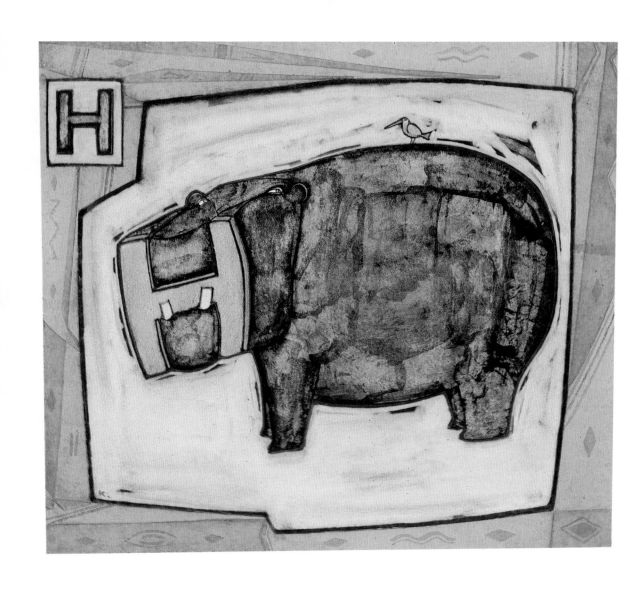

HIPPOPOTAMUS

IGUANA

JELLYFISH

KANGAROO

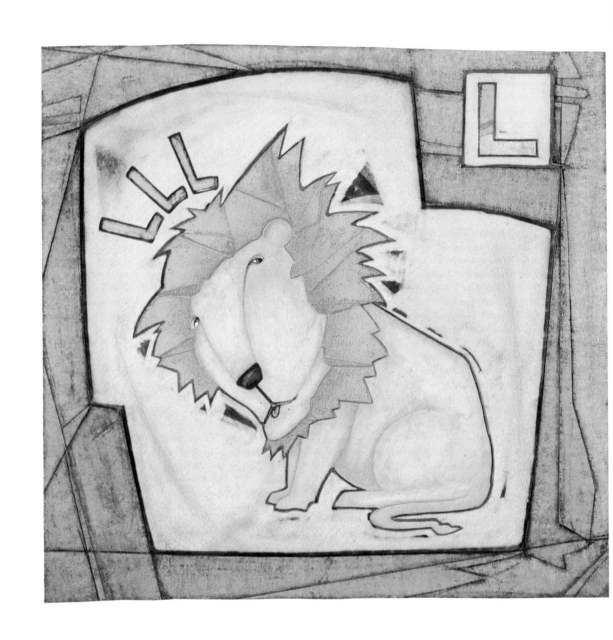

LION

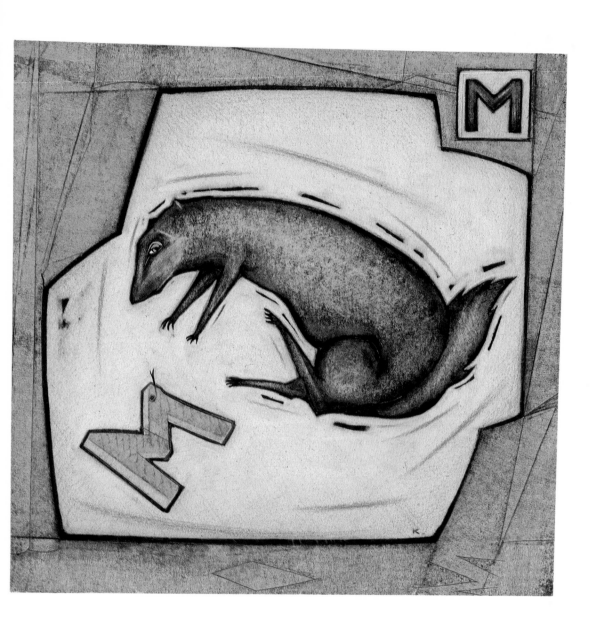

MONGOOSE

NIGHTINGALE

OSTRICH

PANDA

QUAGGA

R HINOCEROS

SEA HORSE

TIGER

UNICORN

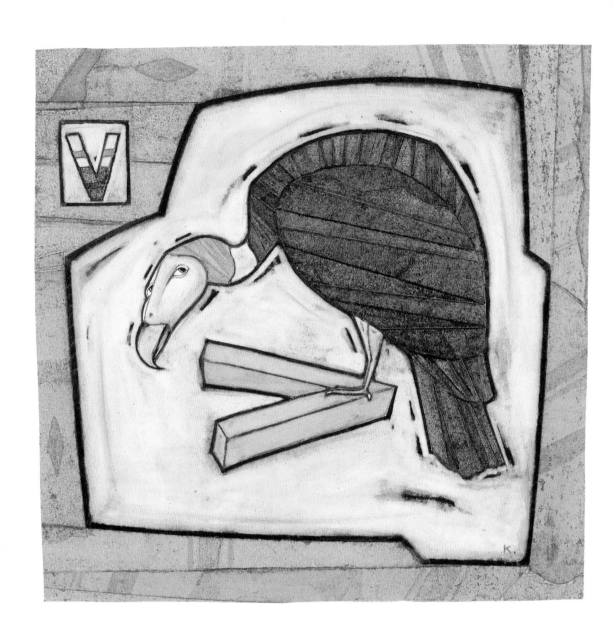

VULTURE

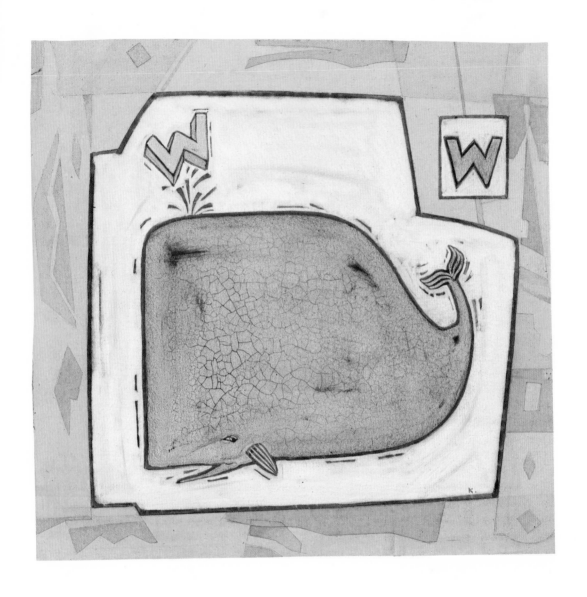

WHALE

X-RAY FISH

YAK

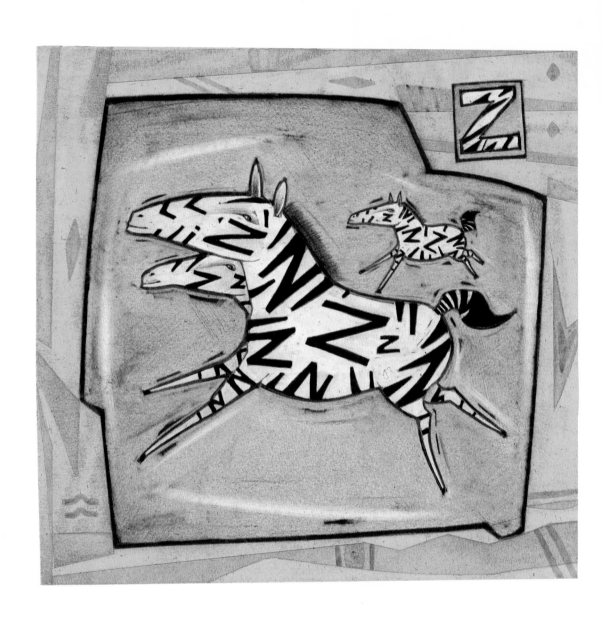

ZEBRA

421
K

Knaff, Jean Christian

Animal characters

$13.95

421
K

Knaff, Jean
Christian

Animal characters

$13.95

DATE	BORROWER'S NAME	

© THE BAKER & TAYLOR CO.